LYDIA BECKER
A CAMEO LIFE-SKETCH

BY

MARION HOLMES

Published by Left of Brain Books

Copyright © 2021 Left of Brain Books

ISBN 978-1-396-32110-8

First Edition

All rights reserved. No part of this publication may be reproduced, distributed, or transmitted in any form or by any means, including photocopying, recording, or other electronic or mechanical methods, without the prior written permission of the publisher, except in the case of brief quotations embodied in critical reviews and certain other noncommercial uses permitted by copyright law. Left of Brain Books is a division of Left of Brain Onboarding Pty Ltd.

Table of Contents

The Nursery of Ideals.	1
The Pioneer Women.	2
The Leader of Votes for Women.	3
Her Early Days.	3
Interest in Science.	4
A Visit to Germany.	4
Honours from the Horticultural Society.	5
Her Training School.	6
The Rising of the Tide.	6
Women's Part in the Building of Empire.	7
A Growing Stream.	8
The First Petition——An Historic Roll.	9
Then——and Now!	10
Lydia Becker's Initiation.	10
The Petition—and Its Effect.	11
Votes for Women in Parliament——the First Skirmish.	11
The First Public Meeting.	12
"Man," an Epicene Word.	12
The Famous Case of Chorlton v. Lings.	13
Prompt Organisation.	14
Women in the Polling Booths.	15
Baffled,——to Fight Again.	15
"Heroism."	16
The First Votes for Women Paper.	16
Deceivers Ever!	17
The "Fairy Princesses" Theory of Mr. Chamberlain.	17

Educating the Electorate.	18
Demonstrations of Women Only.	19
The Great Betrayal.	20
History Repeating Itself in 1912.	22
Save Us From Our "Friends."	22
A Parliamentary Committee.	23
Reaping the Harvest.	23
Unpaid Hewers of Wood and Drawers of Water.	23
Difficulties and Divided Counsels.	24
Some Reforms Won.	25
Work on the Manchester School Board.	26
Her Recreation.	27
A Busy Pen.	27
Last Hours, and a Lonely Journey.	29
The Last Number of The Women's Suffrage Journal.	29
Fit for the Kingdom.	30

LYDIA BECKER A CAMEO LIFE-SKETCH

The Nursery of Ideals.

It is rather the fashion nowadays to scoff at the woman of the early and mid-Victorian period as a timid and foolish creature given to swooning on the slightest pretext, and the victim of a mysterious pride in physical delicacy and weakness. Probably the average woman of the fifties and sixties was not quite so strong and self-reliant as her sister of to-day. The average man still held to the "clinging ivy and the stalwart oak" ideal as being the best and most natural relation between the sexes, and the average woman, with the deeply ingrained habit of making herself pleasing to man, humoured him by no doubt often exaggerating her weaknesses and masking her strength.

But "God Almighty made the women to match the men" in those days as in all others, and the intellectual and patriotic men of the mid-Victorian era had no lack of help-meets fit for them: great souled women who helped to foster and bring to a vigorous youth the comparatively new-born babes of progress and reform.

The Pioneer Women.

What a magnificent roll-call of names rings down from the fifties and sixties! Names of pioneer women who set valiantly to work to clear the ground of the weeds and rubbish of centuries, and with infinite perseverance to beat out a path to a juster and fuller existence for their sex.

One after the other the citadels of education, science, art, social service, politics were attacked, and one after the other—with the exception of the last——the portals of these jealously guarded male monopolies were grudgingly opened. The weapons of abuse, misrepresentation, and personal ill-usage were all freely used against the women in the fight, but they glanced harmlessly off the shields of courage and a high, unfaltering purpose that the last-century Amazons bore. Verily, there were giants on the earth in those days——both masculine and feminine——but more particularly feminine.

The very sound of their names sets women's blood atingle to-day with pride in the heritage that has been bequeathed to them by those pioneers. They roll off the tongue like a call to arms! Florence Nightingale, Josephine Butler, Lydia Becker, Sophia Jex Blake, Mrs. Bodichon, Viscountess Amberley, Isabella Tod, Priscilla Bright McLaren. These, and many others equally courageous, have laid down their weapons now, but there are some of their comrades in arms still fighting in the ranks——a very precious possession for the women of the twentieth century——Mrs. Fawcett, Dr. Garrett Anderson, Madame Belloc, Mrs. Wolstonholme Elmy, Miss Emily Davies, Mrs. Haslam—names indeed to conjure with.

The Leader of Votes for Women.

Lydia Ernestine Becker was pre-eminently the leader: of the Women's Suffrage Movement during its early years. It was her judgement—more than any other perhaps—that moulded its policy, and brought this hotly contested question from a stage of general contemptuous scorn to that of an equally general respect for its inherent justice.

She was born on February 24th, 1827, at Cooper Street, Manchester, and was the eldest of fifteen children——a typical nineteenth century family. Her father, Hannibal Leigh Becker, was of German descent, his father, Ernest Hannibal Becker, being a native of Thuringia, who came to England when quite a young man, and settled in business in Manchester. Her mother was a member of an old Lancashire family, the Duncofts of Hollinwood.

Her Early Days.

The first few years of Lydia's life were spent in Manchester, but when she was still very young the family moved to Altham, near Accrington. They lived in a large house on rising ground, with a fine view of Pendle Hill, and in this beautiful country home the greater part of her life was passed. There was an interval of some years during which they lived in Reddish, where Mr. Becker had calico printing works, but they went back again to Altham.

"Our life at Reddish was a quiet and uneventful one," writes one of Miss Becker's sisters "in the midst of lovely scenery and flowers. The agitations in the political life of the period to some extent affected us. I remember the excitement when it was thought the Chartists might find their way to our peaceful valley; also the year of revolutions, 1848, when Louis Philippe landed in England as 'Mr. Smith.' And the stormy discussions connected with the Anti-Corn Law League were reproduced in miniature in our juvenile circle!

Interest in Science.

"In 1850 we moved from Reddish back to Altham. The drives and walks about presented great attractions to us, as the scenery was on a bolder, grander scale than that round our pretty valley at Reddish. Lydia entered with zest into the study of the plants of the neighbourhood. I remember her pleasure in finding some which were new to her."

Botany and astronomy were always her favourite studies; as a friend of her youth expressed it, "Lydia knew and loved every little flower that grew." The intense delight in nature cultivated during those years in the country remained with her all her life—a never-failing source of pleasure and interest. "In the midst of the anxieties of her political work in London," writes Dr. Helen Blackburn in her *History of Women's Suffrage*, "she found her best refreshment in a run down to the gardens and conservatories at Kew. Visitors to the office could always know when Miss Becker was in residence by the flowering plants she always gathered round her."

A Visit to Germany.

In 1844——when she was about seventeen——Miss Becker paid a long visit to relatives in Germany. I have had the privilege of reading the letters that she sent to her home circle during that time, and they show that she possessed even at that age unusual powers of shrewd observation and reflection. The stilted language of the period in which they are written, probably makes a lack of humour and the serious bent of her mind more obvious than they would otherwise be. She frequently expresses keen appreciation of the beautiful scenery with which she was surrounded, but, on a holiday jaunt, when the heads of most girls of her age would have been filled with thoughts of pleasure and amusement, she wrote home asking for "political news." "I miss the newspapers more than all the English comforts put together," she said.

Honours from the Horticultural Society.

"When she returned home to Reddish, at the end of the year 1845, a great bonfire was kindled," writes Miss Esther Becker. "Soon after her return she began to give us lessons in German. As a teacher her powers were remarkable; she seemed to go right down to the bottom of things .... In 1862 (I think), she won the gold medal from the Horticultural Society of South Kensington for the best collection of dried plants made within a year. She adopted the plan of drying the plants very quickly under great pressure and in heat. The competition was open to the United Kingdom. Her pleasure in botany was intense, and her knowledge of it thorough and complete. She had some interesting correspondence with the celebrated naturalist, Mr. Charles Darwin, in connection with some facts that she had observed in the course of her studies."

Her Training School.

In 1865, the family went to live in Manchester, and a year or two later Miss Becker tried to rouse other women to share the keen pleasure that she had found in scientific studies. She started a Ladies' Literary Society for the study of literature and science, but the results were not very encouraging, the number of members being very far short of her hopes.

All these quiet years of study and effort, however, were fitting her for the post that she was to fill in the great movement that was then attracting the attention of all the thoughtful women of the country. Her scientific pursuits had developed a scrupulous accuracy and attention to detail that proved invaluable in her organising work. They had also strengthened her naturally great intellectual ability and given her a sense of proportion that enabled her to value vexations and disappointments, hopes and wishes at their true worth in the general scheme of things—a very necessary qualification this for one who was to adopt a cause of which disappointments and rebuffs, treachery and trickery were to become the distinguishing features—as time has abundantly proved!

The Rising of the Tide.

For many years——ever since the days of Mary Wollstoncraft, in fact, who published her *Vindication of the Rights of* Women in 1792——isolated individuals of both sexes had tilted a lance in the cause of women's emancipation; but they were few and far between.

The passing of the Reform Act in 1832, however, stimulated women's attention to the power and value of the vote. The substitution in that Act of the words "male person" for "man" in the earlier Acts, first placed women under a *statutory* disability. Before that the franchise had not been barred to them—by law; only by the bar of non-usage. But now the custom of discouragement and disparagement that had been insidiously working for some centuries to press women back from all interest in public duties, was legalised. The prevalent idea that politics was not woman's business was ratified by Act of Parliament.

Ideas and opinions, however, have a disconcerting habit of ignoring Acts of Parliament, and many causes and events were conspiring at that time to overthrow that insulting fallacy.

The Anti-Corn Law agitation, which welcomed the co-operation of the "political nonentities," and the Anti-Slavery movement, did much to show women how deeply they were concerned in politics, whatever the legislators might say.

Women's Part in the Building of Empire.

Then in the fifties came the Crimean War, with Florence Nightingale's magnificent vindication of the ability of her sex to perform great Imperial tasks; and the Indian Mutiny, proving the sufferings and torture of women to be part of the terrible price paid for Empire. Legislation, too,——as always with advancing civilisation——began to interfere more and more in the intimate concerns of the people. (The Divorce Act, which legalised a different moral standard for the sexes, was passed in 1857.)

All these happenings drew thoughtful and public-spirited women together; they began to voice their discontent, and the first ripples of the stream of agitation for the right to vote, that has since spread over the land like a river in spate, began to disturb the political world.

A Growing Stream.

In the sixties the question assumed a certain Parliamentary importance. John Stuart Mill—a keen and tried friend of women—was elected to Parliament in the General Election of 1865, although he took the unprecedented action of including Woman's Suffrage in his election address. Various societies for the furthering of women's interests sprang up, and petitions representing the injustice of the law respecting the property and earnings of married women, and begging Parliament to take the matter into consideration, were signed by thousands of men and women all over the country. *The Englishwoman's Journal* was floated, and Barbara Leigh Smith——afterwards Mrs. Bodichon——and Miss Emily Davies (the two founders of Girton College), Miss Beale and Miss Buss (the founders of the Cheltenham Ladies' College and the North London. Collegiate School respectively), Miss Garrett (now Dr. Garrett Anderson), Miss Jessie Boucherett, Miss Helen Taylor (stepdaughter of Mr. J. S. Mill), Miss Wolstenholme (afterwards Mrs. Wolstenholme Elmy) and others, were agitating for opportunities for the higher education and the opening of further occupations to women. They formed what was known as the Kensington Society, and were keenly alive to the importance of the suffrage.

The First Petition——An Historic Roll.

In 1866 all politicians were absorbed in the proposed Reform Bill, which was to extend the franchise to house-holders. It seemed to women suffragists that this was an excellent opportunity to press their claim to inclusion in the ranks of citizens, particularly with such a champion as John Stuart Mill in the House of Commons. A working committee of well-known women was formed to promote a Parliamentary petition from their sex. They consulted Mr. Mill about it, and he promised to present it if they could collect as many as a hundred names. In a little over a fortnight they had a roll of 1,499 signatures, which included such distinguished names as Florence Nightingale, Harriet Martineau, Frances Power Cobbe, Mary Somerville, Josephine Butler, Anna Swanwick, Lady Anna Gore Langton, Florence Davenport Hill, Lilias Ashworth, Caroline Ashurst Biggs, Anna Maria Fisher (Mrs Haslam), etc. Miss Becker used to say that there should have been 1,500 signatures—hers should have been there. But it was not until a few months later that she became actively associated with the movement.

The story of the handing over of this petition to Mr. Mill has been told many times, but it will bear repetition. In June, 1866, Miss Garrett and Miss Emily Davies took the portentous roll down to Westminster Hall. The size of it embarrassed them so they made friends with the old apple woman whose stall was near the entrance, and she hid it beneath her table. Mr. Mill was nowhere to be seen, but Mr. Fawcett, who happened to pass at that moment offered to go in search of him. When Mr. Mill arrived he was much amused to find the petition hidden away, but the large number of names that it contained delighted him, and he exclaimed "Ah! I can brandish this with effect!"

Then——and Now!

This quiet beginning of one of the greatest agitations in history forms a sufficiently piquant contrast to the great demonstrations for Votes for Women that have taken place in the last few years. Did those two eminent women have visions, I wonder, of the days when they would see London's grey streets aswing with banners, and echoing to the tramp of an army the like of which has never been seen in the world before? Did Miss Garrett——who fought so strenuously to open the doors of the medical profession to her sex——picture the band of medical women, hundreds strong, who marched through London to the tune of the Women's Marseillaise? And had Miss Davies, who laboured to win higher education for girls——any prevision of that army of fair girl graduates in cap and gown, at whose approach men doffed their hats and cheered?

What a gratifying sight those processions must have been to the women who laboured in the early days; thousands, where they had counted tens; a road beaten flat by the tramp of many feet where they had stumbled painfully over the rocks and stones of prejudice and contempt; an army of women of all trades and professions, white-capped nurses, teachers, gymnasts, writers, artists, actresses, marching to overthrow the last stronghold of the most obstinately contested citadel of all!

Lydia Becker's Initiation.

It was at a meeting of the Social Science Association held in October, 1866, in Manchester that Lydia Becker came into touch with the Cause, with which from that time forward she was to be so strongly identified. She was one of the audience when Mrs. Bodichon read a paper on *Reasons for the Enfranchisement of Women*, and she immediately threw herself heart and soul into the work.

The Petition—and Its Effect.

John Stuart Mill presented the petition alluded to above on June 7th, 1866, and organisation crystallised quickly on the heels of the interest that it aroused. Five important societies were formed almost simultaneously in London, Manchester, Edinburgh, Bristol and Birmingham. At a meeting held by the Manchester Society on February 13th, 1867, Miss Becker was appointed Secretary. It was soon recognised that great advantage would be gained by forming some kind of federal union, so in accordance with a resolution passed by Manchester in November, 1867, the five Societies federated, and formed the nucleus of the present large and influential National Union of Women's Suffrage Societies, which is fortunate enough still to retain the presidential services of Mrs. Fawcett, one of the original members of the Committee of the first London Society.

Votes for Women in Parliament——the First Skirmish.

Mr. Mill's hands were strengthened by two further petitions presented to the House before he moved his famous amendment to the Reform Bill of 1867. One petition was signed by 1,605 women householders, the other was from the general public and contained over 3,000 signatures.

The amendment, "to leave out the word 'man' in order to insert the word 'person' instead thereof," was moved on May 20th, in what was universally conceded to be a forcible and eloquent speech, but it was defeated by a majority of 123.

The First Public Meeting.

On April 14th, 1868, the first public meeting for Women's Suffrage was held in the Assembly Rooms of the Free Trade Hall, Manchester. It was the first meeting in this country addressed by women. The chair was taken by Mr. Pochin, the Mayor of Salford, and the resolution demanding "Votes for Women on the same terms as they are or may be granted to men" was moved by Miss Becker, seconded by Archdeacon Sandford, and supported by one who bears a name that is now world famous—Dr. Pankhurst. Meetings in Birmingham and other large centres followed and steady headway was made in winning support in the country.

"Man," an Epicene Word.

But the greatest interest centred round an incident in the struggle that must be reported at some length. By the defeat of Mr. Mill's amendment the word "man" had been retained in the Reform Act. This gave rise to an interesting point of law which can best be described by some selections from Miss Becker's letters on the subject. "The Act of 1867 has struck out the words 'male person' from the electoral law" (these words had been inserted by the Reform Act of 1832, it will be remembered), "and substituted the generic term 'man,' which even in its ordinary grammatical sense is epicene, and requires something in the context to restrict it to the male sex——*e.g.*, 'God made *man* in His own image; male and female created He them.' Here the word man means both sexes of man." But there exists an Act of Parliament (Lord Brougham's Act, passed in 1850), which provides that "in all Acts, words importing the masculine gender shall be deemed and taken to include female unless the contrary be expressly provided." It is not sufficient that the contrary be implied or understood, it must be expressly provided. No such provision is found in the Representation of the People Act of 1867. Accordingly the ratepaying clauses of the Act, which throughout use masculine pronouns, are applied to women ratepayers. Now we maintain that if the ratepaying clauses touch women who are ratepayers, the voting clauses must also comprehend them."

Mere "lay" persons will be prepared to admit that this seems a perfectly sound and logical conclusion; but the minds of Parliamentarians and Lord Chief Justices move by mysterious ways to amazing conclusions——as every-day experience proves.

The Famous Case of Chorlton v. Lings.

The Manchester Committee resolved to test the validity of the women's claim to become voters on the grounds stated above, and steps were taken to get women ratepayers on the register. Miss Becker led the campaign with the greatest zest. A house-to-house canvas of women householders in Manchester was made, and 5,346 women sent in their claims to the revising barristers; 1,341 in Salford, 857 in Broughton and Pendleton, 239 in Edinburgh, and a few more in other parts of the country followed suit. The revising barristers declined to allow the claims in a good many instances, so in order to get a legal decision four cases were chosen for appeal, and were argued before the

Court of Common Pleas on November 7th, 1868, before Lord Chief Justice Bovill and Justices Willes, Keating, and Byles. Counsel for the appellants were Sir J. D. Coleridge and Dr. Pankhurst. This case was technically known as "Chorlton *v*. Lings."

The Second Annual Report of the Manchester National Society for Woman's Suffrage says:——"Sir John Coleridge, in a long and elaborate argument, spoke in favour of the ancient constitutional right of women to take part in Parliamentary elections. He produced copies from the Record Office of several indentures returning members to Parliament, the signatures to which were in the handwriting of women. The right thus exercised had, he contended, never been taken away by statute. He also contended that the general term 'man' in the new Reform Act included women, not only generally, but specifically, under the provisions of Lord Brougham's Act of 1850. Judgment went against the women, however, the judges ruling that they had no statutory right to be recognised as citizens until that right was expressly conferred on them by Act of Parliament."

Prompt Organisation.

There was a General Election in progress at the time this suit was being tried, and on the day following the decision every candidate for Parliament received a letter signed by Miss Becker asking him if he would support a Bill giving votes to women on the same conditions as men if returned to Parliament. Thus the first note of agitation throughout the country sounded simultaneously with the announcement of the decision.

Women in the Polling Booths.

This ruling that the word "man" in an Act of Parliament included woman when it was a question of paying taxes or other duties, but not when it was a question of exercising a privilege, did not affect the few cases where the revising barristers had allowed the women's claims. With characteristic promptitude Miss Becker sent a circular to all whose names were on the register, urging them to vote, and some score of them did. so. Indeed, on polling days in Manchester and Salford she was kept busy taking women voters to the booths; and "their votes," she says, in a letter to Miss Boucherett, "were eagerly competed for by the opposing candidates."

Baffled,——to Fight Again.

After this interesting contest, which proved that there was no chance of getting the suffrage as a side issue, or through the ambiguous wording of an Act of Parliament, the women settled down to a steady campaign of arduous work. Large meetings were organised in all the big industrial centres. In 1869 Miss Becker went on her first lecturing tour to Leeds, Newcastle, and other Northern towns. It proved to be the beginning of a long series, for there is hardly a town of note in the kingdom in which she has not lectured at some time or other. "She was the cleverest, calmest, best balanced speaker the movement has ever produced," says Dr. Helen Blackburn; "one who always seized the salient points, who always got at the kernel of the matter." "Her public speaking was marked not only by extreme clearness of utterance," says another account of her powers of oratory, "but by its lucid statement of fact, its grasp of subject, and logical force."

It was in this year, too, that Mrs. Fawcett gave her first speech on the subject at the first Woman's Suffrage meeting held in London, on July 17th, 1869. Other speakers came forward as time went on: Mrs. Ashworth Hallett, Miss Taylour, Miss Agnes McLaren, Miss Rhoda Garrett, Miss C. A. Biggs, Lady Anna Gore Langton, and Miss Jessie Craigen became notable orators.

"Heroism."

It required considerably more courage in those days for women to get up and speak in public than it does to-day, it must be remembered. Our sex has become perhaps a little too glib in these later years of agitation; at least, one cannot imagine a resolution of thanks to women for their "*heroism* in giving such able and interesting speeches," such as was passed at one public meeting in the seventies, though I daresay some nervous and inexperienced speakers would still consider it applicable!

The First Votes for Women Paper.

In March, 1870, the first number of the *Women's Suffrage Journal* was issued. Lydia Becker was appointed editor, and acted in that capacity to the end of her life. She spared neither pains nor anxious labour to make it what it is——a wonderfully exact record of every step of the movement during the twenty years it was published. The leaders,——showing political acumen and a knowledge of Parliamentary procedure rare even amongst old Parliamentarians,———were written by her. From the first it proved to be an invaluable tie between the Societies that were then springing up in different parts of the country, keeping the workers in touch with each other and giving the cue to their common policy.

The first issue bore testimony to the value that was at that time attached to petitions. When it was started, 20,166 signatures had been sent up to Parliament; but before the end of the Session of 1870 the number had risen to 134,561, and this total was increased year by year until the grand total of 415,622 was reached in 1875. Undoubtedly, the *Women's Suffrage Journal* helped largely to bring about this result by its constant spurring on to effort, and its faithful record of work accomplished.

Deceivers Ever!

The first Women's Suffrage Bill was introduced by Mr. Jacob Bright and passed its second reading on May 4th, 1870, by 124 to 91. The motion to send the Bill to Committee, however, was defeated by 220 to 94.

Mr. Gladstone was in power at the time, and instead of permitting freedom of action to his followers he forbade them to vote with Mr. Bright when "support of the principle" had to be translated into "deeds not words." Having the well-disciplined party consciences of most M.P.'s, they obeyed the dictates of their leader in preference to those of conviction and honour; and the precedent they then established has been, on the whole, faithfully followed ever since.

The "Fairy Princesses" Theory of Mr. Chamberlain.

It would be amusing——were it not so serious in its consequences to women———to see how the "Antis" of those days indulged in the same flowers of oratory as those with which we are so familiar to-day. Mr. Austen Chamberlain had his prototype in the Parliament of 1870 and the caustic comments made by Miss Becker in the *Women's Suffrage Journal* after the debate would be just as applicable to a speech made by the right hon. gentleman in the present year of grace. "To us it appears that the notions regarding women entertained by the opponents of the Bill resemble very closely those of the Knight of La Mancha. They decline to regard women as ordinary mortals, they place them on an ideal pedestal, invest them with imaginary attributes, and base their arguments on the assumption that women are exempted from the rough trials and burdens of life. They refuse to recognise the real Dulcinea at her washtub, they see only the ideal creation of the crazy Knight's disordered brain. We must, however, ask honourable members to come down from the cloudy regions of romance, and to deal with plain, prosaic facts. Our Bill does not concern imaginary Dulcineas but hard working women, who, by daily toil of hand or brain, earn their daily bread. It directly affects a large proportion of the industrial population of this country who are, to use a noted expression, 'flesh and blood.'"

Educating the Electorate.

The Parliamentary story of the cause between the two Reform Bills of 1867 and 1884 is a monotonous one of defeat and disappointment. Eleven debates took place in the House on various Bills and Resolutions between those two dates but, with the exception of the first Bill in 1870——which, as already stated, passed its second reading,——there was a constant, though varying, hostile majority.

Nothing discouraged the women, however, and vigorous propaganda was carried on all over the country in the spirit of "better luck next time!"

Needless to say Lydia Becker was the indefatigable centre round which the majority of the activities circled. Organising, speaking, writing innumerable letters and articles, keeping her finger on the pulse of Parliament and public opinion, she was a notable tower of strength to the movement. Not a single constituency in England escaped her attention, and if the member were averse to Women's Suffrage she promptly organised meetings and activities there.

In 1872 the most important sign of progress was the formation of a Central Committee in London. Representatives of the various Committees in the provinces composed it, and it proved a useful agent for keeping the various Societies in touch with each other and with Parliamentary activities.

In 1873 one hundred large public meetings were held during the first six months, and Miss Becker spoke at twenty-one of them. A yearly average of 200,000 signatures was presented in petitions, and an average of two meetings a week was held in the country during each year of the seventies. Important Conferences took place in Birmingham and other centres, and superhuman efforts were made to return friends of the cause to Parliament.

Demonstrations of Women Only.

In 1880 a series of Demonstrations of women only was successfully organised. The first was held in the Free Trade Hall, Manchester, on February 8th. Others were held in London, Bristol, Birmingham,

Bradford, Nottingham, Sheffield and Glasgow; and Miss Becker appeared and spoke at each one of them. Indeed, the idea of having these great women's demonstrations originated with her, and was first broached in a letter to Mrs. McLaren in 1879. "I am sure when the right time comes for such a demonstration," she wrote, "we could organise in the Free Trade Hall such a grand demonstration of women citizens to demand the Parliamentary vote as would not be unworthy to rank with the Liberal demonstration held in the city to-day, and that without the aid of great men's names to draw them."

"The attempt to fill that immense building by an appeal to one-half of the population, and that the stay-at-home half," writes Miss Blackburn, "was an undertaking that might well make her tremble at her own conception. So strong were her doubts that, two or three days before the event, she went to the hall to see whether, if need be, some portions might be screened off. But when the day came there was no need for screening off——far from it. Instead, it became necessary to provide room for an overflow meeting."

The Great Betrayal.

A Liberal Government was again returned to power in 1880, and the extension of the suffrage figured prominently in their programme.

These Demonstrations of women far eclipsed any that were held by the agricultural labourers for whose benefit, and in response to whose presumably urgent demand, the new Reform Act was to be drafted, and the hopes of the women in the speedy success of their efforts ran very high.

As the time approached for the introduction of the Bill, the Suffrage Societies bent all their energies to securing support for an amendment that would include women in the proposed extension. Resolutions favourable to women's suffrage were proposed at all the large gatherings of both political parties. The Parliamentary Reform Congress, the National Liberal Federation, the National Union of Conservative Associations, the National Reform Union and other representative bodies all carried them by large majorities.

A letter signed by many representative women of the day, including Florence Nightingale, Lady Verney, Mrs. Fawcett, Florence Davenport Hill, Frances M. Buss, Sophia Bryant, B.Sc., Elizabeth Blackwall, M.D., and others equally well known, was sent to every member of Parliament. A memorial stating that no measure for the extension of the franchise would be satisfactory unless it included women, was signed by 110 members of Parliament, and presented to Mr. Gladstone——but all in vain! Though he had in the intervening years apparently repented of his opposition to Mr. Jacob Bright's Bill in 1870, and given a qualified approval to the principle, when the Reform Bill was brought forward in 1884 and Mr. Woodall proposed an amendment that the words importing the masculine gender should include women, Mr. Gladstone vehemently opposed it. "The Bill had as much as it could carry"——"Woman's Suffrage would overweight the ship."——"I offer it the strongest opposition in my power," he said, "and I must disclaim and renounce responsibility for the Bill, should the amendment be carried."

As a result of this strong lead on the part of the Prime Minister, 104 members broke their pledges, and flung them in the faces of the women of the country apparently without any sense of shame or compunction. Such is the pie-crust nature of M.P.'s promises when given to the politically impotent.

History Repeating Itself in 1912.

In spite of this disgraceful treatment of their just demands, I doubt if a single suffrage worker in those days imagined even in her bitterest moods of disappointment and disgust that twenty-eight years hence still another Reform Bill,——giving the vote practically to every boy of twenty-one in the Kingdom——would be introduced without including woman in its provisions. Or that, after the most self-sacrificing and devoted services to the political parties, and an agitation that has carried the cry of Votes for Women from John o' Groats to Land's End, they would still be asked——by another obdurate "Liberal" Prime Minister——to enter the lists of citizenship by the side track of a private member's amendment——if they can!

Save Us From Our "Friends."

Naturally the blow dealt by the betrayal of the supposed friends was a very heavy one, for every extension of freedom amongst men leaves woman in a worse position than before, as she is faced with a bigger electorate to convert and influence.

There was another General Election in 1886. It seemed for a time as if the Cause were about to regain lost ground rapidly, for at that election the number of "supporters of the principle" returned was the highest yet known, being an absolute majority of the whole house. Their support, however, was of the usual lukewarm kind. "The time was not yet ripe," and no occasion for debate was secured until 1892.

A Parliamentary Committee.

In 1887 a Parliamentary Committee was formed, chiefly owing to Miss Becker's exertions, with Mr. Walter B. S. McLaren as Secretary on the Liberal side. Miss Becker acted as Parliamentary agent for the National Societies, and became a very familiar figure in the Lobbies. She was never admitted to the deliberations of the Committee, but had to wait until the meetings were over, and then the secretaries handed over their minutes to her. That absurd custom has been broken down in these later years, and women delegates now are invited freely to sit on Parliamentary Committees.

Reaping the Harvest.

The Suffragists during this Parliament had to content themselves with dull, patient spade work. Sometimes it seemed as if all their work had been in vain, and had to be done over again. But that was not the case. The strenuous labours of the early years were bearing a good harvest——a harvest which, by the way, politicians hastened to reap to their own advantage. Women were no longer outcasts from the educational strongholds; they had a more cultured and wider outlook than their immediate predecessors. In their struggle for political freedom they had received an excellent education in contemporary politics; they were good speakers and organisers——all qualities that could be used in party politics.

Unpaid Hewers of Wood and Drawers of Water.

The Reform Act of 1884 had made paid canvassing illegal and party agents were at their wits' end to get the large amount of clerical and other drudgery connected with elections done.

Politicians were not willing to share with women the power of the vote but they were quite ready——nay, keenly anxious——to welcome them to a fellowship in unpaid political work. Politics no longer degraded women! Canvassing, clerical work, party propaganda——all these activities were truly womanly——"designed to gild your future years with sweet remembrances," according to Mr. Gladstone——so long as they were undertaken in men's interests——not in women's! So the great party organizations, the Women's Liberal Associations, the Primrose League and the Women's Liberal Unionist Associations came into being.

Difficulties and Divided Counsels.

The further history of the Women's Suffrage Movement does not come within the scope of this inadequate review of Lydia Becker's life work. The end came to her activities in 1890, but early in 1888 symptoms of loss of vigour had distressed her colleagues. The movement was then passing through a specially difficult time of depression and loss of hope. Naturally the formation of the party Associations had tended to draw some of the strength and solidarity from the Suffrage Cause, and its enemies were quick to say that it was losing ground; It was inevitable when there was no Bill before the House to act as an incentive to enthusiastic work, that the movement should slacken a little, and funds fall off; defections and divided counsels followed as a matter of course These features combined to bring anxiety on the responsible leaders of the movement, more particularly Miss Becker, who felt very keenly the divisions with her old friends and co-workers.

"Deep affections lay under her stately and reserved demeanour," says Dr. Blackburn. "Her massive force of purpose made her strong to endure, and made pettiness of thought an impossibility for her. Her standard of work was very high, and she exacted the best from herself and from those under her. She had keen appreciation for work well done, but if she met with anything like deceit or underhand dealing she showed no toleration. These were the qualities that drew the strong to her. The fussy and self-opinionated shrank from her. The weak might feel overpowered in her presence, the over-zealous might be disconcerted by her cool reception of their zeal, but those who had power to appreciate power, appreciated her, according to the measure of their own power."

Some Reforms Won.

Women had a longer and tougher fight before them than they realised when they embarked on the struggle for political freedom and equality. The end has not come even yet, but considerable progress has been made in women's emancipation, and Miss Becker happily lived to see some return for her labours. Women were given the municipal vote, the seats of learning were opened to them, education was extended freely, and the right to sit as members of Poor Law Boards of Guardians and School Boards was granted to them before she passed away.

Work on the Manchester School Board.

It was in 1870 that the first great Education Act was passed and women became eligible to serve on the newly formed School Boards. Lydia Becker stood as an independent candidate for the first Manchester School Board and was elected, receiving over 15,000 votes——an eloquent testimony to the respect in which she was held in her native town. She was returned at every subsequent election, and was a member at the time of her death. In spite of her constant activities in the Women's Suffrage movement she took an important part in the work of the Board, and naturally specially interested herself in the provision of educational facilities for girls, and the improvement of the position of women teachers. Mrs. Ashworth Hallett, in an appreciation of her work in The *Woman's Suffrage Journal*, says:

"None can imagine how earnestly she longed to see, as she expressed it, 'the Suffrage out of the way,' in order that she might turn her energies to work for great national questions. Her influence with the working classes was undoubted. She always spoke in an easy practical manner which made the 'masses' believe her to be thoroughly disinterested and true. When the canvassers in the hard fight for the Manchester School Board Elections brought in their result, *both* sides reported 'the working men always say they must keep some of their votes for Lydia.' Thus it was, she received so many votes that she once laughingly said she was far more the 'representative for Manchester' than any of the members of Parliament, because far more electors voted for her than for any of them."

In 1887, at the request of the Board, she laid the foundation stone of the Burgess Street school for girls. She took a keen interest in the subject of night schools and instruction in cookery and nursing for girls, and one of the last matters in which she assisted the Board was the appointment of a Lady Superintendent to supervise the instruction at a girls' night school in sick nursing, dress making, cookery, and laundry work. No wonder the *Manchester Examiner and Times* said at the time of her death, "Manchester is the poorer by the loss of a most estimable citizen, who devoted herself to public service with honesty and ability."

Her Recreation.

Miss Becker apparently took her recreation in what would prove to be to most people an arduous and serious task. I have previously alluded to her love for the scientific studies of botany and astronomy, and this love brought her the greatest delight of her life, participation in the meetings of the British Association. The only occasion on which Miss Becker took a rest of any duration from her editorial and secretarial work was when she went in the autumn of 1884 with the Association to Canada.

On several occasions she read papers before them, and generally took part in the discussions. One that she gave at Norwich in 1868 provoked a good deal of attention and controversy. It was on "Some Supposed Differences in the Minds of Men and Women in Regard to Educational Necessities." Certainly the title seems to hint that it would prove provocative of many varying opinions!

A Busy Pen.

Besides the arduous work involved in the editorship of *The Women's Suffrage Journal*, Miss Becker's pen was often busy for the Cause in other directions. She had a gift of clear and lucid expression that could make even accounts of Parliamentary procedure interesting and intelligible.

She published her first book in 1864. It was a clear and explicit little treatise on *Botany for Novices*. It was not a financial success, however, and that was probably the reason why a companion volume on *Elementary Astronomy* was circulated in manuscript only. In 1867 an article of hers on *Female Suffrage* in the *Contemporary Review* made her name widely known. In 1872 she published a pamphlet on *The Political Disabilities of Women*, and another in 1873 on *Liberty, Equality, and Fraternity——a Reply to Mr. Fitzjames' Strictures on the Subjection of Women*. When she went with the British Association to Canada she contributed a series of descriptive letters to *The Manchester Guardian and Times*.

Naturally, Women's Suffrage in her articles was like King Charles' head in Mr. Dick's——it cropped up continually. The following quotation from an article in *The Manchester Examiner* on "Recreation for the People" is so characteristic of her and still so applicable that I cannot resist the temptation to quote it:——

"The root of the evil of demoralising entertainments lies in the contempt and degradation of women and womanhood, and nothing will cure this evil so long as the law denies to women the full rights of human beings, the power and protection of citizenship. The purification of society is to be looked for, not through repressive legislation, but through the change which will come over men's minds when they shall have learned to look upon women as political and social equals."

Last Hours, and a Lonely Journey.

Lydia Becker died on July 18th, 1890, at Geneva, and was buried there in the cemetery of St. George. She had gone abroad to take a course of baths at Aix-les-Bains. This did her so much good that she decided to extend her journey into the Savoyard Alps. The news of her death fell with a painful stun of surprise on her friends and co-workers everywhere, for her letters home had given accounts of a steady improvement in health.

The record of her last hours was in full accord with her life. She was seized with the malady of the throat that proved fatal when she was staying at Gervais-les-Bains, and when it was at its worst the local doctor told her that the only hope lay in the greater skill of a doctor in Geneva—40 miles away.

After calmly concluding all her business arrangements, she started on the long drive to seek life or face death. Even on that dreadful journey her enjoyment of the beautiful did not forsake her, and several times she called the attention of her attendant to the beautiful scenery by signs, for the disease had bereft her of her power of speech. Arrived at Geneva, the doctor whom she wished to consult was from home. She was taken to the Clinique Juillard, where the matron saw the urgency of the case, telephoned for a doctor and did the utmost for her comfort. Within a few minutes after his arrival, sitting in a chair, the valiant soul passed quietly away.

The Last Number of The Women's Suffrage Journal.

The following notice appeared on the black-bordered cover of the *Women's Suffrage Journal* for August, 1890. It explains itself.

"For twenty years and four months this journal has received the impress of one hand and one mind, so that its long row of volumes form one continuous work, and now when that careful hand is laid low and the energies of that far-seeing mind are carried far beyond our mortal ken, it would seem the most fitting course to close these pages where Miss Becker left them, so that the journal shall be wholly hers, nor suffer by change to any less experienced hand or any mind less comprehensive."

"The loss of her guiding spirit lay heavily on the work everywhere. The Manchester Committee was for a time as a body paralysed," to quote once more from *The History of Women's Suffrage*. "To members of Parliament, to the general public, and in every place where the question was alive, she had been the visible head of the British movement."

Fit for the Kingdom.

Lydia Becker takes an honourable place in the ranks of the "good and faithful servants," for she did what came to her hand without fear or faltering. Having put her hand to the plough she never looked hack, though the furrow she ploughed was a long and strenuous one, and it was not given to her to see the full fruition of her labours. But that the seed that was sown on that laboriously prepared ground by her and her co-workers will come to a full and glorious harvest as surely as the dark shall give place to the light of day we all know; and knowing it, honour her, and give her grateful thanks.

www.ingramcontent.com/pod-product-compliance
Lightning Source LLC
Chambersburg PA
CBHW020432010526
44118CB00010B/538